Me Verses Me

Satish Warrier

BookLeaf
Publishing

India | USA | UK

Copyright © Satish Warrier
All Rights Reserved.

This book has been self-published with all reasonable efforts taken to make the material error-free by the author. No part of this book shall be used, reproduced in any manner whatsoever without written permission from the author, except in the case of brief quotations embodied in critical articles and reviews.

The Author of this book is solely responsible and liable for its content including but not limited to the views, representations, descriptions, statements, information, opinions, and references ["Content"]. The Content of this book shall not constitute or be construed or deemed to reflect the opinion or expression of the Publisher or Editor. Neither the Publisher nor Editor endorse or approve the Content of this book or guarantee the reliability, accuracy, or completeness of the Content published herein and do not make any representations or warranties of any kind, express or implied, including but not limited to the implied warranties of merchantability, fitness for a particular purpose.

The Publisher and Editor shall not be liable whatsoever...

Made with ❤ on the BookLeaf Publishing Platform
www.bookleafpub.in
www.bookleafpub.com

To thee who writes through me

Acknowledgements

I would have remained within myself
Thanks for dragging me out
Preeti,
Anjali,
Aditi,
Marty and Loki (My furry angels)

Preface

In these verses
I battle myself
I will eventually win
when I will lose myself

50 Shades of Me

I Started Now

I started now
I am already late
The very first step
made me feel great

Where were you
For so very long
with a pat on my shoulder
asked, my own fate

I looked in awe
Not recognising
Not even in imagination
my own destination

Regaining composure,
I told him, upfront and straight
Taking the first step was difficult
For ages, I lay in wait

What then, he asked,
made you come awake
A random ripple, I replied
in the placid lake

Cramped with inaction
Blue skies in still water, looked so true
Turned and twisted by the ripple
It tore open the eyes, clamped shut with glue

In the light that dazzled
The sky curved down to the lake
The vivid dome of blue colour
Painted, just for my sake

There I began
to paint the rainbow
Stretching up, to touch the sky
standing on my toes

I started now
But I am not very far
Just a twinkle away
from my shining star

I am the world within

Locked
in a house
nowhere to go
'Alone'

Doors latched
from the inside
Clammed and rusted
'Stuck'

And then
Suddenly alone
hope slipping away
'Drained'

Seconds take longer
Time creeps
Yet it ticks
'Loud'

It's getting darker
Curtains mask the sun
Light loses its shine
'Black'

This locked house
is my mind
I must open my eyes
'Now'

Let the sunshine
Reflect the blue sky
and the happy white cloud
'Bright'

Let the breeze flow in
With the morning smell
Of roses and wet grass
'Soft'

The world out there
and the world within
Filled with glowing light
'Same'

Windows open wide
Doors kept ajar
I am the world
'Within'

Red Tail Lights

In the static river of
Red tail lights
The car stereo
dutifully plays

my playlist,
it knows
so very well

The songs
queue up
Like the seat-belted
Sea of humanity
trapped
in their steely bubbles
With their highs and lows

Some
silently waiting
Some
honking in vain
The traffic creeps
Time creeps too
And… the red tail light glows

The insignificant 'Me'

In a desert
so vast
All I could find
was the insignificance of me
And that
Turned out to be
pretty significant

Scary Tree

It stood
on the street
since the time
it wasn't even a street

The street wasn't a street
A lonely desert track instead
It stood there alone
where the very habitation ceased

Knotty, knobby
Menacingly evil
Spooky
To the very least

Making noise
of eerie wind
through its hollows
Like a hungry beast

It's outstretched
dried branches
Clawed on the trembling hearts
Till, they let out a shriek

It preyed
on the lonely travellers
Innocently carrying their wares
to the village across the creek

Those were its hay days
when it ruled
Weary days and naughty nights
of trick or treat

But that was the past
Way before yesterday
Much different
From the today and now

The streets are now full
Busy and loud
The tarred road uneasily cramped
And the shops vedged on either side

Its branches, scraped
on the concrete sides
The erstwhile claws
Cut to its humble size

It still made the eerie sound
faithful remained the breeze
In the din of the traffic
it wasn't more, than even a wheeze

In the march of humanity
Even the ghosts never dared
The tree scared a few back then
But now,
everyone was already scared

Ashes to Ashes
(Tanka Poetry)

Fire rises from spark
with its fury and shine
Unrepentant flame burns all that it touches
destroying itself too
Remorselessly

It blazes fiercely
Feasting on wood and air
In ravenous hunger, it devours itself
Dies as it consumes
There remains the ash

Ashes, white and grey
For that is what it was
The essence of the burning wood, air and
fire
In its blazing glory
And it's smoking calm

They dance to my Music

I gaze out
head resting
on the window
Loyal window glass
letting in the sun
yet holding off
the deafening cacophony
My car speeds up
My music plays
I watch outside
And see the world
dance to my music

The glitz and the glare

The glitz beacons
unblinking eyes stare
It isn't what it seems
When laid out stark bare

So I fly
to those faraway skies
Where there remain no shapes
Just the streaks of glorious light

Comfortably soaring
above the shine and sparkle
Where there are no truths, no lies
Merging without a bind or a shackle

From there, I dive
glowing and aware
Unaffected now
By the glitz and glare

Wrinkles tell tales

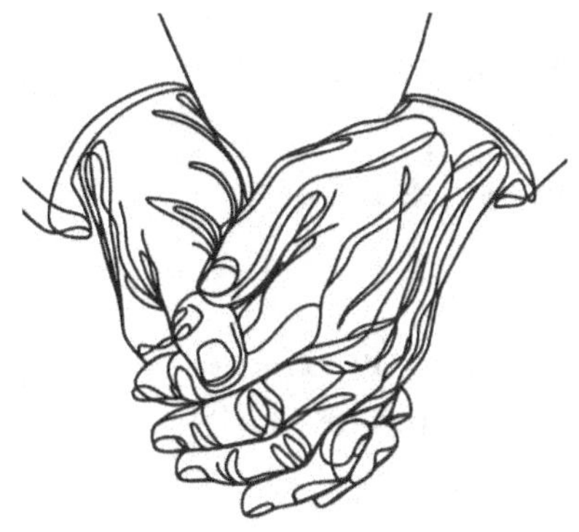

Wrinkles
tell many tales
Silently waiting
Willing to be told
Age slowly creeps
Till it's finally old

Tales of every beach visited
Salty, lazy and sunny
Lying there, without a care
and the mountains climbed
Wrapped, seeped and immersed
In crisp cold air

Of warm, shining sun
Floating on the flimsy mirage
Creating illusionary glow
of floating raindrops
reflecting the splendour
In a vivid, arching rainbow

Of pain
Excruciating or mild
Winced yet endured
Of wounds
Fresh and old
Some raw, some cured

Spoken
only to the resonating hearts
That feel.
Spoken
Only to the fingers
That heal

Wrinkles
Tell many tales
Silently waiting
Reflecting on the greying eyes
Memories weep
Blending the apparent truth
and the obvious lies

Strapped to the seat –
Safe

Cool breeze caressing my face
through the open window
brings a smile to my weary lips
as I see the passing meadow

Singing merrily in celebration
of the moment, I waited for so long
The beat of the track on the rail
Forming the rhythm of my song

Emotions reach a crescendo
as the locomotive chugs past the stream
Heart beats faster
Forming an unheard scream

The small cottage on top
Wins my heart
Alas, I am homeward bound
From the very start

The view so dear, oh so enchanting
naughty stream
skipping over rounded stones
I am so sure, I want to be there
but to jump would mean broken bones

The plush seat, the cosy blanket
Lure you to stay back
The window grill forewarning the gruesome
fall
Making you step back

Making you hesitate
for a moment of time
Long enough to commit
the sinful crime

To be scared
Letting go of a dream
allowing to be trapped
In a cage, comfortable as may seem

Letting the moment pass by
staying on the speeding train
Letting go of a lifetime
scared off by a momentary pain

Even before you tried
afraid you would fail
Onward you stay as a passenger
on a preset trail

Cool breeze wiping a tear
from the forlorn eye
Across the grilled windows
As the meadows pass by

Bliss in the arms

In this big world
We are only two
And you know what
That's the only truth

The stars so many
twinkle they do
The sun and moon
There are only two

Who needs anyone
Us are just enough
Need no long list
Just You is enough

There is bliss
In your arms
That's beyond the world
If,
you only knew

Little hands hold the world

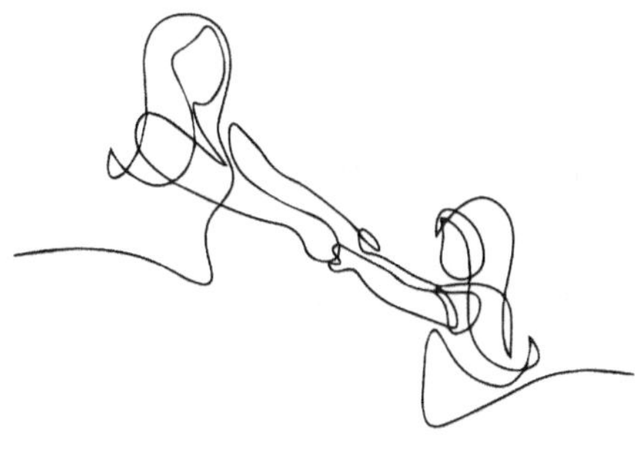

Little hands
Holds the world
it ain't big
But then it's everything

It brings smile
on her lips
And it smiles
Right back on her

There lies
In those eyes
All the joy
The world can bring

It's immense
Beyond words
Unmeasurable
That feeling

And I hold
The infinite in my hand
it ain't big
But then it's everything

The colour just lies in my eyes

The sky turns
Orange and blue
What was pitch black
in the night

It's the light
which owns the colour
Absence of it
Makes it night

The sky
Colourless and limitless
The colour,
stays trapped in my eyes

So when I see
the sky turning dark
I just need to close my eyes
and see it sparking bright

A dot

●

A dot
Single,
unidimensional
and bare.
It lies marked
Dark and filled
on a paper
empty,
white and fair

It could be
the start,
It could be the end
with nothing furthermore
Or it could be
all that, there can be
And
nothing more

It holds within
every line

It could be a part
Yet be
None of them
It is a dot
which is yet not a line
or a circle
a square
or the weirdest trapezium

It is away
from none
till there isn't
a second one
And if there is another
then a possibility
of a line
has just begun

But to join the dots
is a choice
Once joined, however
all dots are aligned
Unlike a line
stuck in two dimensions
the dot
has no plane, no bind

This moment of now
is a dot in time
Holding the future
and the trailing past
Yet all by itself,
it holds
the possibilities
Infinitely vast

So hold the Now
Before
you draw the line
For the choice lies there
of everything else, there is
In every dot
In every now

There I know I am

My skin is wrinkled
My touch is still warm
There I know
I am

My voice is feeble
My songs still echo
There I know
I am

My eyes have blurred
But my dreams are vivid still
There I know
I am

My hands tremble
I hold you close still
There I know
I am

My heart is weaker
It still has you in it
There I know
I am

Deep inside
and somewhere between you and me
There I know
I am

The itch that lives in my head

I scratched the skin
And found the blood
The persistent itch
Stays forever in my head

I am screaming
Without a sound
To seek an echo
Nowhere to be found

The steps in frenzy
walk out of line
A straight line
A straight-jacketed line

And outside it all
there is a space
of crazy flying saucers
setting the town ablaze

Of flying men
defying the gravitational laws
And Kryptonite stone
accentuating their flaws

In those mad dreams
that I saw with my eyes wide open
I found the voice,
speaking the language of the chosen

I then wander in search
till I find there is none
In the crowd, I realise
I am the only one

There, it will all
come around
Homeward bound
Homeward bound

Then, in a final scratch
I pierce the dead
To be the itch
That lives in my head

Bathed in my own glow

There is a strong urge
to shine
But before that
I need to glow

I need to see
for myself
What I intend
to show

I must grind
the edges
till they are
amply sharp

It may cut through
the hide
But it must
pierce the heart

Words must weigh
because
they need to
sink deep

It must hurt
Enough
to make
the eyes weep

I can wait...
till forever
Across
many lives

For something
so profound
I won't compromise

It's the truth
I have to say
and none other

And when I'm ready,

I wouldn't need
No words to utter
I will need no spotlight

When I am bathed
in the light
Of my own glow

The petal and the Dew

The petal
that held
a drop of dew

None would last
None will remain,
forever new

But for now
A beautiful blend
of the divine two

Blending
the fragrance of the flower
And the freshness of dew

If the petal
were to be worried
of withering

And the dew
was aware
of its own disappearance

They would miss
The sun
Shining on the dew

And the fragrance
wafting
happily through

And then
The magic
would be over

And
the moment
would be lost forever

The rights and the wrongs

The right and the wrong
The shackles unseen
the iron bars
and the gaps in between

Together they mark the bounds
of the solitary prison cell
In such confines
Exists the life, we know so well

The cells separate the prisoners
One from the other
Confined in their respective cells
Till the time reaches forever

The bars they say
keep the prisoners safe
to keep them alive
in their own confined space

The gaps allow
the stretch beyond the rim
Only far enough
till the iron bars tear the skin

It's not only the bars
That keep you in.
It's also the gaps
That never lets you win

The rights and the wrongs
Together they bind
To be free
It's the beyond that I need to find

It's not the bars
I need to bend
It's not the gap
that I need to pretend

It's me that's in the trap
It's the me that needs to melt
When I cease to be in the cell
there are no gaps, no bars to be felt

In the empty cell
There remains only a song
and me resonating, on either side
Of what is right and what is wrong

A glimmer escapes

What should I wear
to hide myself
Isn't the skin enough?
It keeps me wrapped up
Encased
Entrapped

What should I wear
to save myself
Isn't this tough hide enough?
It keeps me protected
Armoured
Cocooned

What should I wear
to be accepted
Isn't this colour correct?
It keeps me camouflaged
Uniform
Blended

What should I say
to be heard
Isn't the scream loud enough?
It keeps me in tune
Silent
Muffled

Yet the glimmer escapes
a glimpse of what can be
Isn't that what can't be hidden?
It keeps me hopeful
Praying
Waiting

Words need not Rhyme

There she stood
on the vast stage
Playing her part
A mere word on the page

Audience spot
what they want to see
Each eye seeing a part
For me, it was 'She'

For each masterpiece
there is an eye
For her performance
Beholder am I

Orchestra plays
Weaving the symphony
Each note blending
Some true, some phony

Who applauds
Who appreciates?
For whom is it worth
what each one creates?

No one notices
Yet we seek the gaze
An affirmation,
Some words of praise

Her eyes shifts
from one to another
Seeking a connection
a friend or a brother

Each stare is stony
Each eye cold
No nods to acknowledge
No hands to hold

Till she finds mine
Her eye wanders
Her own warmth
in her quest, she squanders

She sees herself
in my eyes
In her own glow
she feels nice

Word realises
It's own meaning,
this time
And when it realises,
It doesn't need to rhyme

I need a bath

I need a bath
Soap and froth
Spray of water
A scrub and wash

Body weary
Full of grime
Heart laden
With hate and crime

Some I like
Others I hate
Cage of destiny
Bind of fate

Happy moments
Brings a smile
Sad ones follow
After a short while

Full of anguish
String of regrets
Missed opportunities
And some lost bets

I carry the burden
Memories from the start
Furrows on the forehead
Worries in the heart

In the holy,
One dip I yearn
to unshackle the web
Many things to unlearn

I run the water
Bring up the froth
Scrub clean the weary skin
Emerge free, pure at heart

Smile on the Window

Window seat
head on the glass
Engine revs up
Road moves
Trees run in haste
houses slower in background
road turns fuzzy black
Trees a blur of green
Cruising the wind
Homeward bound
On the window glass
I see a smile

I seek the Whole

I am half,
Incomplete
I search,
For what, I know not

I am hungry
Famished
I seek
The claps, I get not

I am guilty
Ashamed
I confess
For a crime, I did not

I am lost
Wandering
I set course
To a destination, I know not

I seek
My whole
In all those eyes
My within, I see not

Lake lies in wait

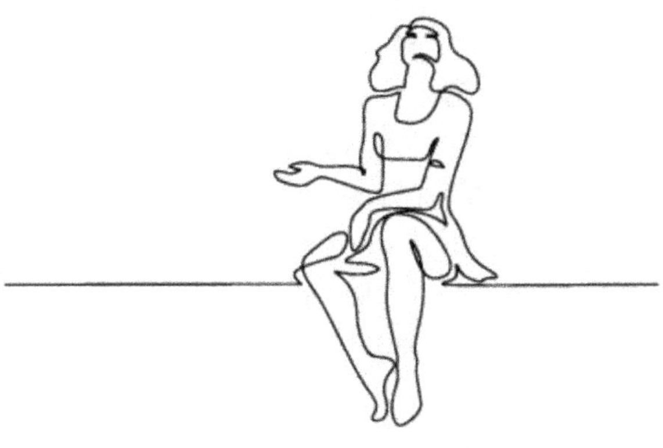

Rain falls
from heaven
a subdued trickle sometimes
or an angry downpour otherwise

On the hard pavement
making sound
Or landing softly
on the wild grass around

Creating a din on the noisy roof
Or knocking intrusively on the window pane
They all trickle down
onward each drop moves without refrain

Driven by an unseen attraction
they gather and greet
Through the rivulets and drains
some filthy, some neat

Waking the sleeping puddle
with a splash tad sloppy
Creating ripples faraway
on the obscured blue canopy

Flowing along merrily
Keeping afloat the paper boat
Crafted with innocent hands
fuelled by imagination and hope

Umbrellas of many colours
Dangle on youthful song
Sometimes shielding the rain
Sometimes just playing along

Playful and gay, streams tumble
humming the common lore
Following the beaten path unaware
carved by many streams before

Rivulets join the lake
the end is here
Some wait at the banks
The unknown they fear

Rivulets and streams so many
The lake is just one
Drops don't remember a thing
Wise lake remembers each one

It's raining now
soon the sun will adorn the skies
From the placid lake
essence of the clouds will soon rise

Rain falls from the skies
The heaven does so create
Who knows where it falls
The sun and the lake, lie in wait

How dead is the grass

How real is the world
How real is the dream
Is it the one I heard
Or is it the one I have seen

Which one do I believe
What I see or what is shown?
In my mind, the forest grows
New seeds each day is sown

The weeds are as much the forest
As much are the flowers and trees
so are the crawlers and the big cats on prowl
the mammoth, the birds and the tiny bees

One is eaten and the other survives
In the jungle, the strife is perpetually on
Stealthy paws and nervous hooves spar
Grass gets trampled by both, forest lives on

In this melee, I wonder
Where does the truth rest
How dead is the grass?
How alive is the forest?

Closer to my core

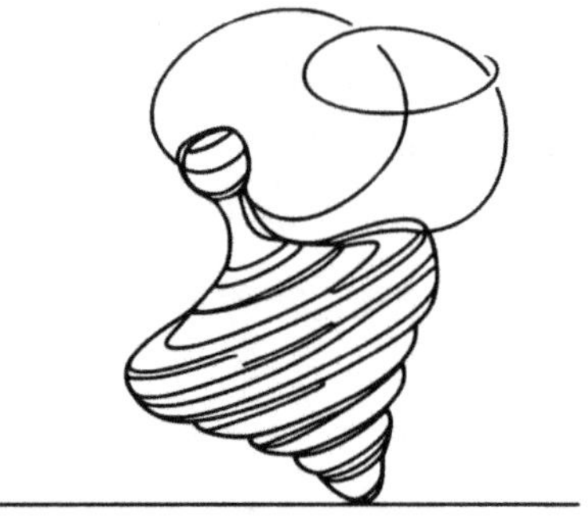

Like a top
constantly in motion
Edges moving faster
slowly moves the core

If I would stop
I would fall
Fearful of not spinning
Afraid, of being 'me' no more

On pointed end
I hang in balance
Forever in pursuit
drilling through the floor

Force of the chord
would eventually expire
Inevitable would happen
spinning top would spin no more

With the last wobble
the top falls
It lays down on its sides
no longer on its toes

As I lay down calm
spinning no more
My being was still
Closer to my core

Backseat

Sometimes
One must take a backseat
Bit messy
not particularly neat
Watching the travelled path
roll out through the rear window
Reflecting on the past
and not worrying of the future
Watching the sun
peek through the passing trees
Shading the half-open eyes
sleepy but not tired
Hands free, off the steering,
but instead
folded on the resting neck
supporting the relaxed head
Legs on the window
No longer on the peddles
No longer urging for speed
or ready to press the brakes
No longer in control
of the music console
Listening to
whichever song that gets played

Waving to people
Spreading smiles, not rage
Waiting for the next ones to come
as each of them move off the stage
Sometimes
You deserve to chill
Moving at your own pace,
as per your own will
Sometimes, you must pause
and enjoy the treat
Sometimes
One must
take a backseat

Awake or Dreaming

Bad dream
plays out
Torments
behind the closed eyes
Cold sweat
on the brow
and a pounding heart
That almost died

Woke up
relieved
It was unreal
made up with a bunch of lies
Awake now
dream yet lingered
fading yet laden
With a list of whys

Unreal t'was
but the fear wasn't
Limits of reason
It brazenly defies
I try and forget
and sleep again
unable to shed the memory
despite the eager tries

There I lay
staring at the dark
Afraid of my own mind
of what it can conjure and fantasise
Half asleep
or half awake
Drifting in between
the fretful mind
and the tired eyes

I had a dream

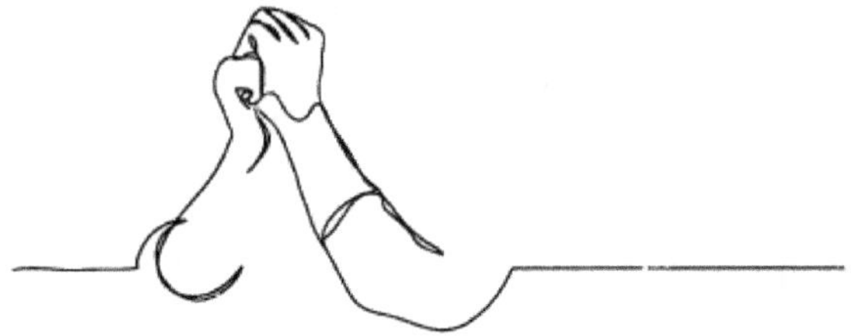

I had a dream
that glazed my eyes
as a wide-eyed kid
Unsure and forlorn
A dream,
vague and unclear
Yet wondrous,
hopeful and warm
Of being someone
who, I wasn't yet
And who
I would be, eventually
A dream of reaching
a favourable point
in the stream of time
Gradually, yet surely

And then
with the wonder-struck eyes
And my unsteady little hands
I rowed,
the little boat of mine
Then came the eddies
The boat, they twisted and tossed
till the oars fell off
and the little hands held onto the rails
The boat drifted
along the stream
guided by the currents
and the unforgiving winds
Till it reached
somewhere on the stream of time
A destination
certainly not mine

I should have rowed
Yes, I do regret
But to miss the fun on the eddies
I regret a bit more
I should have left the rails
I should have gotten wet
On the roller coaster ride
in Joy, I should have yelled

Waters are calm now
I am closer to the sea
The tumultuous stream I travelled
I can look back and see
Every path
Every stream, I could see
was flowing quietly
into the vast sea
There, in the boat
enjoying the setting sun
as the river merged into the sea
I quietly stayed
There, in the calm
My wrinkled hands left the rails
Looking up at the sky
Thanking god, I silently prayed

Incomplete

I am half,
Incomplete
I search,
For what, I know not
I am hungry
Famished
I seek
The claps, I get not
I am guilty
Ashamed
I confess
For a crime, I did not
I am lost
Wandering
I set course
To a destination, I know not
I seek
My whole
In all those eyes
My within, I see not

There lies the Music

The flute plays
a melody
soothing and flowing
I wonder,
who owns the song
and where lies the music
The dexterous fingers
playing on the vents
claims the song as theirs to play
The wooden pipe boasts too
of having the requisite length
and the characteristic timber
The mind proclaims
oh so vainly
I am the conceiver,
of those insightful notes
I am the one
who guides those fingers
to play ever so elegantly
But then
there echoed a voice
from the warm depth
of the beating heart
For there, arose that feeling

that rush of ecstasy
of knowing the song
before it was ever heard
For there, flowed the notes
before they could be written
and composed
From there it resonated
in many hearts of those
who heard and felt
the same ecstatic rush
There
In the multitude of pure hearts
resonating with the happy rhythm
where they all sway
in gay abandon
Is where,
the song belongs
And there, I feel lies the Music

The beast

The beast
lurks in the dark
Hiding away
in un-lit shadows
Lashing out
at the saviour's hands
In anger
In fear
Now
it lurks alone
Scary
and scared

The free words

Few words
escaped my clamped cage
grouping together
they climbed up on the stage

They were incited
by the persuasive thought
One that ignited the mind
to go boldly, beyond the taught

In a group
there is a shared courage
Afraid and trembling, no more
they stand together on the stage

Up on the stage
they gather up in a sentence
Speaking loud and clear
Fearlessly breaking the learned pretence

And then they spoke
to the many ears
Some moved, in melancholy
Some shedding customary tears

The thought had moved
It echoed in another mind
The words are resonating
and they are no longer just mine

Out of the cage
In the air
Singing along
Without a care

The unseen dust

Like a stone
I lie still
Unmoving, anchored
by my own burden
My own load
my deep weariness
Thick, dense
Seeped in inertia

There are
Places to go
Paths to be travelled
But they can wait
Till I weather to the dust

Then I will flow
with the happy river
Dissolved in the drops
falling over the precipice
spraying in the wind

Then I will fly
Just a mere dust
 in the air
Unseen
Insignificant
Light like air
And free like the wind

Somewhere between
Earliar and Later

In the rush
of things
the moment stops
somewhere between
Earlier and Later
And that's where
there is no speed
No expectations
No comparison
Nothing lesser or greater
Yet there, lies still
the intent of motion
and the sense of purpose
The seed of every future
a pure slice of the creator
There lies the beauty of stillness
the symphony of motion
Existent, but yet lost
Somewhere between
Earlier and later

The Good and the Bad me

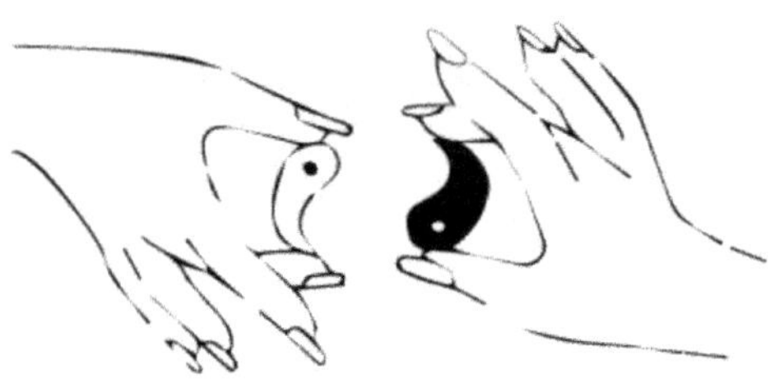

There is good in me
that peeks
and yearns to be seen
There is bad in me
that seeks
to cast its shadow
on the screen
It's not that
the good,
is what is me
And the bad,
is not me
It's just what I choose
to keep,
Is all,
That is me

And there lies the truth

I am falling
Faster and heavier
Pulled inwards
Yet surging out
The tear is wider
Ripping open the truth
Layer by layer
the sheaths are parted
the endless fall ends
Static at the bottom
There in the abyss
in the blinding light

the vision is clear
In the placid mind
there are no sheaths
There is just me
and there lies the truth

In a Happy Place

There was a knot
a hurting one
Deep
within the beating heart
The constricting cage
holding the fear
Piercing
like a painful dart
The dread and the gloom
permeated the core
Stretching
and tearingit apart
At the bottom of abyss
where light ende
motionless
In the abysmal dark
There I lay
away from grace
In despair
hope away from my grasp
In that lonely cold
I felt the gush
of a warm current
A touch of the benign grace

I closed my eyes
felt your warmth
Snuggled
in that warm embrace
There loosens the knot
and the fear is gone
There, I find love
In you, I find faith
There I rise
with warm currents
I feel your presence
watch was masked by despair
In the rise
I know you are here
I know in the fall
You were there too
We may fail to notice
sometime in despair
But in every moment of joy or grief
Our Love is always there
Wherever and however
Irrespective
In your embrace
I know, I am in a happy place

Grown

Little hands
Caressed
Gently ruffled
the worried hair
And in that cosy moment
crept the carefree sleep
like a shroud
on a tired soul
And then
when I opened
my sleepy eyes
She was gone
Grown
And then
I couldn't sleep

I experience the Sin

I experienced
the sin
Pure and septic
Gagged, up to the brim

Through the sieves
of Desires
In the hell
of scorching fires

It flowed
through the veins
Burning the neural path
furrowing deep ruts in the brain

Botched patches
of dried blood
Making random patterns
of the habitual flood

For there was
nothing to gain
Just to experience
The inscrutable pain

Yet it prevailed
Vanquishing the sane
In the duel for reason
a fight in vain

Clouded lights
forming blinded shadows
Crawling the grimy floor
as the spectre arose

Larger than the eye
it could no longer see
Entangled in the long tethers
Conjuring the illusion of free

The divine voices called
Well-meaning, yet irate
Drowning hands clawed the precipice
just in time before too late

In the sweat
I came washed
with trampled skin
Deeply rashed

No clothes could stick
the new naked dawn
Exposed to the dewy rays
the demon was gone

I found the divine
Beyond the din
Blissfully aware
I had experienced the sin

The hug too late

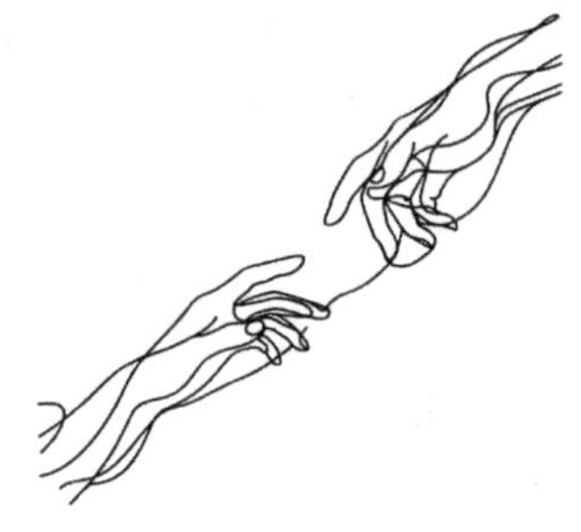

The hug
Too late
Held back
by false pride
One chance was lost
by me
The second
the fate denied
Stony faced
I sat
while I melted within
Inside
Eyes welled
but the tears had dried
Regret weighed on my heart
Unseen, I cried

And then she had grown

Her tiny feet
went beyond the cradle
Kicking away the warm rug
I gently placed it back
and then
She had grown

Her little hands
waved back
She entered the school's gate
I waited a bit longer
And then
She had grown

Her eloquent voice
Recited the poem, nice
She bowed as they clapped
I clapped the loudest
and then
She had grown

Her twinkling eyes
Searched for us
She glowed in glory
There in the crowd
My eyes welled with pride
and then
She had grown

It's her birthday
I whisper wishes to the sky
There far away
she looks up and smiles
And then
She had grown

Lingering ache

If she ran
with her little feet
to give me a hug
I would run back
through time
to reach that spot
Once again
to stay
a little bit longer
Hold her
a little tighter
Fill my heart
with the ache
that would linger
Forever

I am the Sun

The sea
Tranquil and at ease
Aware of the shimmering mirage
on its restless waves
From it's warmth
It felt the Sun

Why? it wondered
And asked the warm one
While you play among my waves
you turn me
Into a cloud
Answer me, oh mighty Sun!

Why? May I ask
Do I drift as a cloud in the breeze
Cover the sky
And mask your light
Turn dark and broody
As I clump into one

Why? Do I split then
into many and fall
Splashing on pavements and grass
just when I was
Happy in a cloud
Having my little fun

Why? Do I suffer
the pain
As I fall as rain
And flow over rocks
Scouring to make my own path
Always on the run

Why? Do I tire
get polluted
by my own doing or of other's sin
I feel sluggish and filthy
When I reach my end
When I am done

There in the end
I am back where I started
Starting from me
Pouring out back into me
I live this cycle over and over again
Aren't you the one to blame,
O mighty Sun

Fiery yet calm
Sun spoke through the rays
of the pristine dawn.
I float in the dark emptiness
Throwing out light
From here, everything I can see
I burn

Holding the raging fire
in my bosom
The turmoil within
In the light and the heat
is there for everyone to see
Oh serene one

Only you
turn into mist
at my touch
The mountains remain
The plants grow
Flowers smile in glee

My fiery rays
feel balmy warm
embraced by all it touches
Some flourish, some wilt
Each one guided
By their nature, none are free

I am not to be blamed
Neither I claim any fame
It's for them to wilt or flourish
I don't nourish
neither punish
It is for me to just burn

You are
the cloud, rain and the river
Wistful, flowing and wet
change is your nature
Yet always
Into the sea, you return

We are both
cursed and blessed
You evaporate
I burn
You are the sea
I am the Sun

On a Forever Journey

A moment
A lifetime
Always together
One step at a time

Sharing a laugh
Shedding a tear
Always in bliss
One step at a time

Celebrations of success
Trepidation of failures
Holding hands always
One step at time

The warm hug
Heartbeats resonate
Always in embrace
One step at a time

A breath
A fragrance
The endless infinite kiss
One step at a time

Friends
Smitten in love
On a forever journey together
One loving step at a time

Let's paint the fence

Fence separates the inside
From what lies outside

It's not for the fence
to judge or decide
It stays on the fringe
In touch with either side

Not the one to connect
Only built to divide
It's one fence
With two sides

One is with the inside
One faces the outside
One side restricts
The other side protects
In its essence
it is meant to bisect

I pick up the brush
Let's paint the fence
I wonder which side to paint first
From where do I commence

From which side is your view
From the side you view
It doesn't belong to either side
It is just a fence

Silent shriek

I shout
Profound
A silent shriek
Sound falls
through the clouds
further deep
Travels forever
No one to hear
Nowhere to echo
Into the abyss
Nothing to hold
None to let go
I hear my shout
Loud in the mind
Silent outside

I will live my life
tomorrow

Weary eyes squint
after an uneasy night
as the unfaithful curtains let in the
unforgiving sunlight,
sips from the bitter cup of coffee
push the dreams to the fringe
ushering in, the real world
fast enough to make you cringe,
Let's get up and run
there's a lot to be done
Today, there's a schedule to follow
Wait,
I'll live my life tomorrow

Hurried footsteps over the grass
fail to notice the drops of dew,
shed by the trampled blade of grass
over the polished shoe
Merging into the milling crowd
losing identity like the flake in the snow
Saying yes
When at times I should've said No
Today this bitter pill
I need to swallow
Wait,
I'll live my life tomorrow

In the everyday din
unheard goes the soul as it screams
Running after the aspirations
we race the clock, forgetting our dreams
So many tasks
so many biddings to be done
Before I think of myself
there are so many accolades to be won
Today let me make a fortune
to save my tomorrow
Wait,
I'll live my life tomorrow

Deceitful mirror be blamed
for my face that did fade
Hidden in the shadows
of the roles that I've played
Tired body rebels
and the weary limbs ache
but it's not over yet
there is so much at stake
Looking at the closing clock
I wish a moment I could borrow
But I am tired and I must sleep now,
Wait,
I'll live my life tomorrow

At last I spoke

A blank page
My mind a turmoil
I've stood watching
A spectator always
as life took me
on a roller coaster ride
All I did was
to hold on to my seat
Never swam
Just flowed by
Didn't steer away
From the set course
Never spoke out
But then,
did I want to be heard
Would I dare
Break the silence
Or just pass by
Without a whimper
Yes I heard myself
Oh how helpless I was
Couldn't even stop myself
But maybe, this is a beginning
At last I spoke

Wake up
Dream no more
Take off the mask
You always wore
It's time we see each other
One within
And the one in the mirror

www.ingramcontent.com/pod-product-compliance
Lightning Source LLC
LaVergne TN
LVHW050915200726
843508LV00011B/2202